YOKAI LORE

AN ILLUSTRATED GUIDE
TO
JAPAN'S DEMONS
AND
GHOSTS

PHANTOM PRESS

Copyright © 2025 by Phantom Press. Revision 2.

All rights reserved. No part of this publication may be reproduced, distributed, or transmitted in any form or by any means, including photocopying, recording, or other electronic or mechanical methods, without the prior written permission of the publisher except as permitted by U.S. copyright law.

For permissions, inquiries, or further information, please contact: phantom@mountain-mill.com

CONTENT

INTRODUCTION	4
AKA MANTO	7
SHŌJŌ	11
JOROGUMO	15
GASHADOKURO	19
KAMAITACHI	23
NURARIHYON	27
AMANOJAKU	31
KAWAUSO	35
TENGU	39
ONI	43
KAWAAKAGO	47
AKANAME	51
KEUKEGEN	55
YOSUZUME	59
BAKENEKO	63
TESSO	67
ROKUROKUBI	71
HITOTSUME KOZO	75
YAMA UBA	79
REFERENCES	82

INTRODUCTION

In the shadowy realm between the mundane and the mysterious dwell the yokai, supernatural beings that have captivated Japanese imagination for centuries. The term yokai itself—combining the characters for "bewitching" (妖) and "strange" (怪)—hints at their complex nature. These entities are not simply monsters or spirits, but rather manifestations of human experience, cultural memory, and the inexplicable aspects of the natural world.

As we journey through these pages, we encounter yokai that span the full spectrum of supernatural existence—from the terrifying Aka Manto haunting modern bathroom stalls with its deadly choices, to the jolly Shōjō whose sake-induced celebrations bring good fortune to the worthy, to the seductive Jorogumo whose beautiful human form conceals a deadly spider's intent. Each represents a different facet of Japan's relationship with the supernatural, showing how these beliefs have evolved from ancient times to the present day.

The yokai presented in this volume reflect the remarkable adaptability of these supernatural entities. As Japan transformed from a rural, traditional society to an urban, technological one, its yokai transformed too. Ancient spirits once confined to remote mountains and forests found new homes in the mundane spaces of modern life—lavatories, city streets, and even the digital realm. This evolution demonstrates how deeply yokai are embedded in Japanese cultural consciousness, constantly reinventing themselves to remain relevant across generations.

The illustrations accompanying these tales pay tribute to the legendary Shigeru Mizuki (1922-2015), whose distinctive artistic style revolutionized the visual representation of yokai in modern times. As a manga artist, folklorist, and cultural historian, Mizuki dedicated his life to preserving and reimagining Japan's supernatural heritage. Through works like his seminal "GeGeGe no Kitarō" series, he introduced yokai to postwar generations, ensuring these ancient traditions would not be forgotten in an increasingly westernized Japan. Mizuki's ability to render yokai with both whimsy and psychological depth—to make them simultaneously otherworldly and deeply human—established a visual language that continues to influence how we imagine these entities today. Our illustrations honor his legacy by embracing his characteristic blend of the cartoonish and the macabre, the humorous and the horrifying.

These stories offer more than mere entertainment—they provide unique insights into both historical Japanese society and contemporary cultural concerns. Through the terrifying moral choices presented by Aka Manto, the celebratory wisdom of the Shōjō, or the environmental justice dispensed by Jorogumo, yokai stories continue to teach valuable lessons about human behavior and our relationship with the world around us. They remind us that supernatural beliefs continue to resonate even in our increasingly technological world, addressing universal human concerns about morality, identity, and our place in the natural order.

As you turn these pages, remember that in the world of yokai, nothing is quite as simple as it appears—beauty can mask danger, terror can serve justice, and the line between human and spirit is often surprisingly thin.

AKA MANTO

THE BATHROOM MONSTER

猩猩

Region of Origin: Urban restrooms throughout modern Japan

Earliest Known Tales: Showa period

Nature: Malevolent, Mischievous

Appearance: Masked figure in a red cloak

Unique Power: Forces victims to choose between deadly options

Danger Level: Highly dangerous—avoid at all costs!

In the most unassuming of places—the quiet privacy of a public bathroom—lurks one of Japan's most unnerving modern yokai: Aka Manto. This eerie figure first appeared in the post-war 1950s, a time when the country was undergoing rapid urbanization. As ancient yokai stories about spirits dwelling in forests and mountains began to lose their relevance in an increasingly urban society, Aka Manto emerged to haunt a location closer to home: public restrooms, especially those in schools.

Aka Manto is not your typical ghost. Cloaked in a flowing crimson cape, the figure hides its face behind a disturbing mask, creating an atmosphere of chilling anonymity. When it encounters a victim, it presents them with a deceptively simple question: "Red paper or blue paper?" This choice, however, carries dire consequences. If the victim chooses the red paper, they are destined for a gruesome fate—bleeding out, their blood matching the shade of their chosen color. On the other hand, selecting the blue paper seals their doom in a different way: suffocation, their body turning a deathly blue as the life is slowly choked out of them.

The only escape from this horrific encounter is to refuse both options, offering a chilling suggestion: sometimes, the best choice is no choice at all. This grim tale reflects the moral tension at the heart of the Aka Manto legend—where every choice comes with a deadly price.

Aka Manto's origin is not merely a coincidence, as it ties directly to the societal shifts happening in Japan during the post-war period. With cities expanding and daily life shifting away from rural traditions, this modern yokai adapted to the changing landscape. No longer confined to ancient temples or dark forests, Aka Manto began to haunt the very spaces where people spent their most mundane moments—public bathrooms. The figure became a symbol of how ancient fears of the supernatural could manifest in the modern world, turning an ordinary bathroom stall into a place of terror.

As the tale spread across Japan, regional variations of the Aka Manto legend emerged. In the Kansai region, the entity became known as "Aka-kami," or "Red Paper," while northern areas told of the "Aoi Manto," or "Blue Cape." Some versions of the story even included different color choices, such as yellow or white, each with its own horrific consequence. These variations show how local adaptations of a story can arise, yet they all share the same central theme of life-or-death choices and their horrifying results.

The influence of Aka Manto has grown far beyond the realm of ghost stories. Today, the legend is embedded in Japanese popular culture, with appearances in manga, anime, and video games. Parents even use the story as a way to keep children from lingering too long in the bathroom, reminding them of the dangerous spirit that could be waiting. Aka Manto is also part of a broader collection of supernatural beings that haunt bathrooms, including the infamous "Toire no Hanako-san," a spirit that also claims public restrooms as its domain. Together, these spirits form a uniquely Japanese tradition—reminding us that even the most ordinary spaces of daily life can be home to extraordinary and deadly forces.

Aka Manto teaches us that sometimes, in the face of danger, the only way to survive is to defy the rules entirely. And in a world where the line between the living and the supernatural is often blurred, it's never wise to underestimate the power of a simple question.

SHŌJŌ
THE SAKE-LOVING SPIRIT
少女

Region of Origin: Coastal regions of Japan, especially near sake breweries

Earliest Known Tales: Classical period, referenced in Noh and Kabuki theater

Nature: Jolly, Mischievous

Appearance: Red-faced, long-haired spirit with a fondness for sake

Unique Power: Can bless worthy humans with endless sake

Danger Level: Generally harmless—unless you try to steal their sake!

From the terror of bathroom stalls, we move to a more convivial corner of Japanese folklore. The Shōjō represents a fascinating example of cross-cultural mythological evolution. The name itself originated from the Chinese word for orangutan (猩猩), but in Japanese folklore, it transformed into something uniquely different—a sake-loving spirit whose red face and hair might recall its simian origins, but whose nature embodies distinctly Japanese attitudes toward alcohol and celebration.

SHŌJŌ

The earliest written accounts of Shōjō appear during the Heian period (794-1185 CE), where they emerged in both Chinese and Japanese texts. Their association with sake-drinking likely developed from multiple sources: the natural connection between red faces and alcohol consumption, the Japanese cultural significance of sake in religious ceremonies, and perhaps even observations of orangutans' ruddy complexions. Over time, these elements merged to create a creature that perfectly embodied the complex relationship between spiritual enlightenment and controlled intoxication in Japanese culture.

Unlike many yokai who inspire fear or caution, Shōjō are generally viewed as benevolent entities. They are most often spotted near the sea, where they dance and sing with seemingly inexhaustible energy, their movements growing more graceful rather than clumsy with each cup of sake consumed. Their sacred brew is said to possess remarkable properties—healing the sick, bringing good fortune, and even granting wisdom to those deemed worthy.

The tale of Taketori exemplifies the Shōjō's role as arbiters of virtue. When Taketori sought help for his ailing father, the Shōjō tested not just his dedication but his character. Only after demonstrating genuine humility and compassion did he receive the magical sake that would cure his father. This story, like many involving Shōjō, suggests that these spirits judge humans not by their status or wealth, but by the quality of their hearts.

The influence of Shōjō extends beyond folklore into traditional Japanese arts. The Noh play "Shōjō," written by the master playwright Zeami Motokiyo (1363-1443), remains one of Japan's most frequently performed traditional dramas. Its complex choreography mimics the fluid, supernatural movements of the drunken spirit, while its distinctive red masks have become iconic in Japanese theater. The play weaves together themes of reward for virtue, the relationship between humans and spirits, and the transformative power of sake.

In modern Japan, the legacy of

SHŌJŌ

Shōjō continues in unexpected ways. Their image adorns sake bottles and brewery signs, their stories are referenced in contemporary entertainment, and their association with celebration and good fortune persists. They remind us that not all supernatural encounters need be frightening—sometimes they can simply be an invitation to join in life's pleasures, albeit with wisdom and moderation.

JOROGUMO

THE SEDUCTIVE SPIDER WOMAN

絡新婦

Region of Origin: Mountainous and forested areas of Japan, such as Joren Falls in Izu

Earliest Known Tales: Edo period

Nature: Seductive, Dangerous

Appearance: Beautiful woman who can transform into a giant spider

Unique Power: Lures men with her beauty and traps them in her webs

Danger Level: Extremely dangerous—run if she offers you company!

While Shōjō embodies the joyful aspects of supernatural encounters, Jorogumo represents a darker, more seductive face of the yokai world. Her very name contains a fascinating double meaning: written as 女郎蜘蛛 (jorōgumo), it means "woman-spider," but the same pronunciation can be written as 絡新婦 (jorōgumo), referring to the golden orb-weaver spider native to Japan. This linguistic duality perfectly captures the creature's dual nature—a being that exists between human and arachnid, between beauty and horror.

The natural world provides the foundation for Jorogumo's legend. The golden orb-weaver spider, *Nephila clavata*, displays remarkable characteristics that likely inspired the yokai's mythology. Female spiders grow significantly larger than males, their webs shimmer with a golden hue in sunlight, and they can reach impressive sizes that capture human imagination. Japanese observers noted these traits and wove them into a tapestry of supernatural belief.

According to traditional accounts, a spider's transformation into Jorogumo follows a specific timeline. After reaching four hundred years of age, the creature gains magical powers. At one thousand years, it achieves the ability to transform into a beautiful woman. This gradual evolution reflects a common theme in Japanese folklore—the idea that time and patience can transform the mundane into the magical, the natural into the supernatural.

The most famous Jorogumo legends come from specific locations across Japan, each adding its own elements to the story. In Nagano Prefecture, near the Joren Falls, tales speak of a Jorogumo who nearly drowned a woodcutter, only to be thwarted by quick-thinking locals. In Gifu Prefecture, the spider woman is said to protect sacred waterfall caves, punishing those who would defile them. Kyoto's stories tell of entire geisha houses run by spider yokai, while Edo-period Tokyo buzzed with rumors of abandoned mansions where beautiful women lured men to their doom.

Perhaps most intriguingly, Jorogumo sometimes appears as a force for environmental protection. In these tales, she punishes those who would harm the forests and rivers where she dwells. Her beautiful human form serves as both lure and weapon, drawing in those who would damage nature and ensuring they never return to continue their destruction. This aspect of her legend has gained renewed significance in modern times, as contemporary Japanese society grapples with environmental concerns.

JOROGUMO

The influence of Jorogumo extends far beyond traditional folklore. Her story captured the imagination of Lafcadio Hearn, whose writings introduced many Western readers to Japanese folklore. Ukiyo-e artists, particularly Utagawa Kuniyoshi, created striking depictions of the spider woman that continue to influence visual interpretations today. In kabuki theater, her transformation scenes provide opportunities for spectacular stage effects that demonstrate the art form's technical sophistication.

Modern Japanese culture continues to find new meanings in the Jorogumo legend. Contemporary interpretations often focus on themes of feminine power, the dangers of superficial beauty, and humanity's complex relationship with nature. Her story serves as a reminder that in Japanese folklore, nothing is quite as simple as it appears—beauty can mask danger, terror can serve justice, and the line between human and yokai is often surprisingly thin.

GASHADOKURO

THE GIANT SKELETON OF NIGHTMARES

がしゃどくろ

Region of Origin: Various regions across Japan

Earliest Known Tales: Post-war folklore, popularized in the 1960s

Nature: Malevolent

Appearance: Giant skeleton towering over trees, with glowing eyes

Unique Power: Can become invisible and silent, crushing unsuspecting travelers in the dark

Danger Level: Extremely dangerous—if you hear ringing in your ears, it's already too late!

Where Jorogumo uses beauty and seduction to lure her prey, Gashadokuro represents a more primal, visceral kind of terror. This colossal skeleton, towering fifteen times the height of a normal person, embodies the collective suffering of those who died from starvation, war, or disaster without proper burial. The name itself,

GASHADOKURO

がしゃどくろ (gashadokuro), evokes the rattling sound of bones, a chilling onomatopoeia that captures the essence of this fearsome yokai.

The origins of Gashadokuro are deeply intertwined with Japan's history of famine and conflict. During the Great Tenmei Famine (1782-1787), entire villages perished, their bodies often left unburied. The Sengoku period (1467-1615) saw countless battlefields strewn with the dead, while natural disasters throughout Japanese history have claimed numerous lives without proper funeral rites. According to folklore, when large numbers of people die under such circumstances, their accumulated spiritual energy and resentment merge, creating these giant skeletal apparitions.

The most unsettling aspect of a Gashadokuro encounter is its subtle warning sign. Victims report hearing a faint ringing in their ears, similar to distant temple bells, moments before the creature appears. By the time this warning registers, it's often too late—the massive skeleton has already spotted its prey. The phenomenon is particularly active between 2 AM and 2:30 AM, a time traditionally known as the "hour of the ox," when the boundary between the physical and spiritual worlds grows thin.

The creature's hunting method is direct and terrifying. Unlike the elaborate schemes of Jorogumo or the playful tricks of other yokai, Gashadokuro simply reaches down with its massive bony hands to snatch up victims, crushing them or biting off their heads with its enormous skull. The size difference between predator and prey makes resistance futile—how does one fight a skeleton the height of a modern office building?

Regional variations of the Gashadokuro legend reflect local histories and tragedies. In northern Japan, tales often connect these beings with victims of harsh winters and famine. Coastal areas speak of Gashadokuro formed from the bones of those lost at sea, their remains never properly recovered and laid to rest. Near ancient battlefields, stories tell of warrior Gashadokuro still bearing the armor and weapons of their mortal

GASHADOKURO

lives.

Modern interpretations of Gashadokuro have found fascinating parallels with scientific phenomena. The ringing in the ears that heralds their approach bears similarities to the effects of infrasound—low-frequency sound waves that can cause feelings of dread and auditory hallucinations. Changes in atmospheric pressure and electromagnetic fields have also been suggested as natural explanations for some of the sensations associated with Gashadokuro encounters.

Yet perhaps the most significant aspect of the Gashadokuro legend is its role as a memorial to historical tragedy. Each bone in these massive skeletons represents an individual who died without proper ceremonies, their spirits unable to find peace. In this way, Gashadokuro serves as both a frightening monster and a powerful reminder of society's obligation to honor and remember its dead. Their very existence calls attention to historical injustices and the importance of treating death with proper respect.

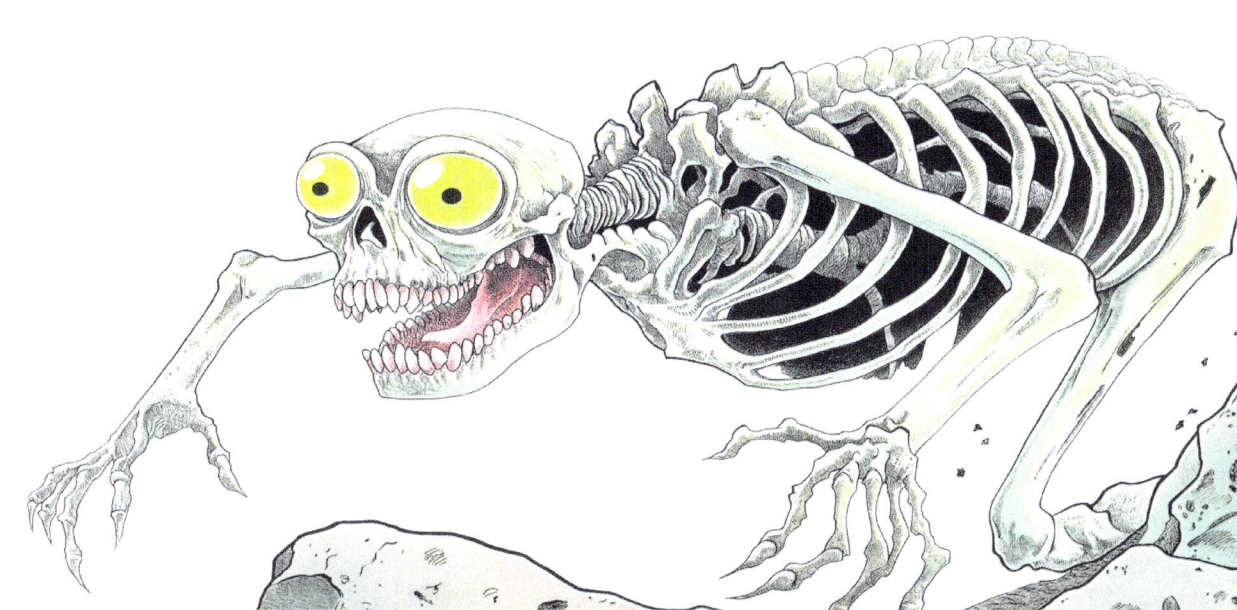

KAMAITACHI
THE WIND-WEASEL TRICKSTER
鎌鼬

Region of Origin: Mountainous and snowy regions of Japan, especially Nagano and Tōhoku

Earliest Known Tales: Edo period

Nature: Mischievous, sometimes Malevolent

Appearance: Weasel-like creature with sickle-like claws, often riding the wind

Unique Power: Attacks victims with lightning speed, leaving painless cuts

Danger Level: Moderately dangerous—watch out when sudden winds blow!

From the towering terror of Gashadokuro, we turn to a more subtle but equally distinctive supernatural threat. The Kamaitachi—invisible weasels riding mountain winds—exemplify how Japanese folklore often explains natural phenomena through supernatural narratives. Their name combines 鎌 (kama, "sickle") with 鼬 (itachi, "weasel"), perfectly describing both their appearance and their peculiar method of attack.

KAMAITACHI

The legend of Kamaitachi probably originated from observations of natural phenomena in Japan's mountainous regions. When strong winds whip through narrow valleys and mountain passes, they can create dust devils and sudden pressure changes. These atmospheric effects, combined with the sting of wind-driven particles and the numbing effect of rapid temperature changes, might explain the mysterious cuts that mountain travelers sometimes discovered on their skin—cuts they didn't notice receiving.

What makes Kamaitachi particularly fascinating is their coordinated method of attack. Unlike solitary yokai, these wind-riding weasels work in trios, each with a specialized role. The first weasel knocks the victim down with a gust of wind, the second uses its razor-sharp sickle-claws to make the cut, and the third applies a mysterious ointment that prevents pain. This elaborate choreography explains why victims only discover their wounds later, finding clean, painless cuts with no memory of receiving them.

Different regions of Japan have developed their own variations of the Kamaitachi legend. In the Kanto region, they're seen as playful tricksters whose cuts are more annoying than dangerous. The Chubu region, with its many mountain passes, views them as more serious threats to travelers. In northern areas, they're known as Kaze no Kami (Wind Gods), while coastal regions call them Matsukaze (Pine Wind), reflecting local environmental conditions.

Historical medical texts from the Edo period mention "wind-cut disease," attempting to explain these mysterious injuries through the medical knowledge of the time. Some texts prescribed specific treatments for Kamaitachi cuts, combining practical wound care with spiritual remedies. These medical accounts demonstrate how supernatural beliefs often intertwined with early scientific understanding.

Perhaps most interestingly, Kamaitachi have evolved from pure threats into unofficial guardians of mountain paths. Their pranks, while startling, often serve to keep humans

KAMAITACHI

from wandering into more dangerous areas. Some legends suggest that their cuts are actually warnings, steering travelers away from treacherous paths or impending storms. This protective aspect reflects a common theme in Japanese folklore—that even seemingly malicious yokai may serve important protective functions.

The influence of Kamaitachi extends into modern Japanese culture in surprising ways. Their name has been adopted into martial arts terminology, describing swift, cutting movements. Meteorologists have studied the wind patterns in areas associated with Kamaitachi legends, finding interesting correlations between reported encounters and specific atmospheric conditions. Even contemporary urban legends speak of "razor winds" in city alleyways, showing how these ancient mountain spirits have adapted to modern settings.

NURARIHYON

THE YOKAI HOUSE-GUEST

ぬらりひょん

Region of Origin: Coastal areas of western Japan, especially Okayama and Hiroshima

Earliest Known Tales: Edo period (1603–1868)

Nature: Mischievous, Invasive

Appearance: An old man with an oversized, gourd-shaped head, wearing elegant robes

Unique Power: Slips into homes unnoticed, acts like the master of the house, drinks tea, and confuses everyone

Danger Level: Socially awkward—lock your doors or lose your snacks!

Moving from the wild mountain winds to the intimate spaces of Japanese homes, we encounter one of the most peculiar yokai in the supernatural pantheon. Nurarihyon's name itself is a subject of scholarly debate, possibly deriving from "nureru" (濡れる, "to become wet") and "hyon" (飄々, "floating freely"), suggesting his slippery, impossible-to-pin-down nature. Unlike the violent Gashadokuro or the trickster Kamaitachi, this yokai's approach to human interaction is uniquely presumptuous—he simply walks into homes and acts as if he owns them.

Nurarihyon emerged during Japan's Edo period (1603-1867), a time of significant social transformation. His appearance—that of an elderly man with an oddly elongated, egg-shaped head, dressed in elegant noble's clothing—reflects the period's complex class dynamics. During this era, traditional power structures were beginning to shift, and the rise of the merchant class was challenging the established social order. Nurarihyon, with his ability to enter any home and command respect through sheer presumption, perhaps embodied both the anxieties and aspirations of a changing society.

The timing of Nurarihyon's visits is carefully calculated for maximum effect. He typically arrives during the evening hours, when families are settling down for dinner or preparing for bed. Walking through the front door as if he belongs there, he takes the master's seat, drinks the household's finest tea, and makes himself completely at home. The most remarkable aspect of his behavior is how it affects those around him—household members find themselves inexplicably unable to question his presence or challenge his authority.

This supernatural home invasion takes on different characteristics across Japan. In some regions, Nurarihyon is seen as a test of household harmony—his ability to infiltrate a home supposedly reveals weaknesses in the family's spiritual defenses. Other areas view his visits as a form of blessing in disguise, believing that homes he chooses to enter will prosper, provided the family handles his intrusion with proper etiquette.

Perhaps most intriguingly, Nurarihyon holds the title of Supreme Commander of all Yokai, a position that seems at odds with his relatively peaceful method of operation. This leadership role suggests that in the yokai hierarchy, power isn't always demonstrated through fear or violence. His ability to command respect through mere presence and social presumption represents a uniquely Japanese understanding of authority—

NURARIHYON

one based on subtle social cues rather than overt displays of power.

The legend of Nurarihyon continues to resonate in modern Japan, where issues of privacy, social boundaries, and proper etiquette remain highly relevant. Contemporary interpretations have linked him to everything from unwanted houseguests to social media oversharing, demonstrating how ancient yokai can adapt to address modern concerns. Some even see him as a commentary on Japan's aging population, as his elderly appearance takes on new significance in a rapidly graying society.

Modern scholars have also noted the psychological sophistication of the Nurarihyon legend. His ability to make people accept his presence through sheer confidence mirrors real psychological phenomena, where social pressure and assumed authority can lead people to accept unusual situations without question. In this light, Nurarihyon might be understood as an early exploration of social psychology, wrapped in supernatural garb.

AMANOJAKU

THE LITTLE DEVIL ON YOUR SHOULDER

天邪鬼

Region of Origin: All across Japan

Earliest Known Tales: Heian period (794–1185)

Nature: Malevolent, Contrarian

Appearance: A small horned imp with a wicked grin and a twisted little body

Unique Power: Whispers bad ideas, stirs up rebellion, and pushes people to act on their worst impulses

Danger Level: Psychologically dangerous—don't listen to that voice in your head!

While Nurarihyon influences human behavior through social presumption, Amanojaku takes a more direct approach to manipulating the human psyche. The name itself reveals deep religious roots: 天邪鬼 combines the characters for "heaven" (天), "evil" (邪), and "demon" (鬼), creating an ironic title that suggests corruption of the divine. This complex etymology hints at the creature's sophisticated role in

Japanese folklore as an entity that explores the darker aspects of human nature.

Tracing Amanojaku's origins takes us back to ancient Buddhist texts, where the creature first appeared as an adaptation of the Sanskrit demon Pāpīyas. As the legend migrated from India through China to Japan, it transformed, becoming less of a purely evil entity and more of a complex trickster figure that reveals uncomfortable truths about human nature. By the Heian period (794-1185), Amanojaku had become firmly established in Japanese mythology, appearing in the Kojiki and other foundational texts.

Unlike many yokai who maintain a physical distance from humans, Amanojaku operates by getting inside people's heads—sometimes literally. Traditional accounts describe this spirit as having the ability to possess humans, but its preferred method of operation is more subtle. It whispers contrary thoughts, encourages rebellion against social norms, and brings out the worst impulses in people. If someone is told to be quiet, Amanojaku urges them to shout. When kindness is called for, it promotes cruelty.

The physical appearance of Amanojaku reflects its nature as an entity that straddles the divine and the demonic. Often depicted as a small, oni-like creature with dark or red skin, sharp claws, and occasionally a third eye, it combines fearsome attributes with a size that makes it seem less threatening than larger yokai. This contradictory appearance—scary yet small—mirrors its role as a being that represents internal rather than external threats.

What makes Amanojaku particularly fascinating is its role in Japanese religious and philosophical thought. Unlike Western concepts of temptation, which often focus on specific sins, Amanojaku embodies a more fundamental kind of corruption—the urge to do exactly what we're told not to do, simply because we're told not to do it. This speaks to deep questions about human nature, free will, and the psychology of rebellion.

AMANOJAKU

One famous legend tells of a woman who tried to outsmart Amanojaku by telling it the opposite of what she wanted, assuming it would make her target do the right thing. This clever plan ultimately backfired, demonstrating that the spirit's contrary nature operates on a deeper level than simple opposition. The story suggests that trying to manipulate or outsmart our darker impulses often leads to unexpected consequences.

In modern Japan, the term "amanojaku" has entered everyday language as a description for contrarian personality types, particularly in children. This linguistic evolution shows how ancient yokai continue to provide vocabulary for discussing human psychology and behavior. Contemporary interpretations have also linked Amanojaku to modern phenomena like social media trolling and reflexive opposition to authority, showing how this ancient concept remains relevant to current social issues.

KAWAUSO
THE PLAYFUL RIVER OTTER SPIRIT
川獺

Region of Origin: Rivers and streams across Japan, especially in rural areas

Earliest Known Tales: Edo period (1603–1868)

Nature: Mischievous, Trickster

Appearance: Looks like a cute river otter, sometimes walks upright and wears human clothes

Unique Power: Mimics human speech to confuse travelers, throws parties in the moonlight with other animals

Danger Level: Harmless but chaotic—don't accept sake from a suspiciously charming otter!

From the psychological manipulations of Amanojaku, we turn to a more lighthearted presence in Japanese folklore. The Kawauso, or river otter yokai, represents a fascinating intersection between natural history and supernatural belief. These shape-shifting spirits evolved from observations of the Japanese river otter (Lutra lutra whiteleyi), a species whose playful behavior and remarkable intelligence captured the imagination of generations before its tragic extinction in the modern era.

The natural behavior of river otters provided rich material for folklore. These animals displayed complex social structures, used tools for hunting, and exhibited what appeared to be joy in their play—characteristics that seemed almost human to careful observers. Their ability to move effortlessly between land and water suggested a creature that could cross boundaries between worlds, while their intelligence and social nature made them perfect candidates for supernatural elaboration.

Unlike many yokai who interact with humans through fear or trickery, Kawauso's approach to human interaction tends toward playful mischief. Their most famous ability—the power to mimic human voices—reflects actual otter vocalizations, which can sound surprisingly human-like. Stories tell of these spirits calling out to travelers in familiar voices, creating confusion that the Kawauso find endlessly amusing. Some accounts even describe them transforming into traveling salesmen, attempting to sell fish back to the very villagers from whom they stole them.

Regional variations of Kawauso legends reflect local environmental conditions and cultural concerns. In Shikoku, they're known primarily as tricksters who steal fish from nets, while Kyushu's traditions cast them as helpful guides who assist lost travelers near rivers. The peoples of Honshu tell tales of Kawauso appearing as merchants in marketplace pranks, and in Hokkaido, they're viewed as protective spirits of rivers and streams. These regional differences often corrclatc with how local communities historically interacted with their waterways.

The complexity of Kawauso folklore deepens when we consider their ability to form genuine friendships with humans. Unlike many shape-shifting yokai who interact with humans purely for their own benefit, Kawauso sometimes develop lasting bonds with those who show them kindness. This aspect of their nature perhaps reflects real observations of otters' capacity for social bonding and their ability to form relationships with humans under certain circumstances.

KAWAUSO

Traditional Japanese culture recognized the significance of Kawauso through various customs and beliefs. Many fishing communities maintained specific rituals to appease these spirits, hoping to ensure safe passage on rivers and successful catches. Some areas even established small shrines near riverbanks where offerings could be left to maintain good relations with the local Kawauso population. These practices reflected a sophisticated understanding of the need to maintain harmony between human needs and natural forces.

The tragic extinction of the Japanese river otter in the late 20th century has added a bittersweet dimension to Kawauso folklore. These supernatural tales now serve as cultural memories of a lost species, preserving ancient knowledge about otter behavior and human-wildlife relationships that might otherwise have vanished. Modern environmental movements sometimes invoke the Kawauso as a symbol of river conservation, using these traditional stories to promote watershed protection and species preservation.

TENGU

THE TRICKSTER OF THE MOUNTAINS

天狗

Region of Origin: Mountain forests across Japan, especially in Kyoto and the Japanese Alps

Earliest Known Tales: Heian period (794–1185)

Nature: Proud, Mischievous, Sometimes Protective

Appearance: Humanoid with red face, long nose, and crow-like wings or features—often dressed like a mountain monk (yamabushi)

Unique Power: Controls wind, teleports through forests, masters of martial arts and illusion

Danger Level: Unpredictable—may teach you sword skills… or dropkick you off a cliff!

From the playful river spirits, we ascend to the mountain realms of one of Japan's most complex and influential yokai. The Tengu, whose name combines the characters for "heaven" (天) and "dog" (狗), has evolved far beyond its original conception as a dangerous dog-like entity from Chinese folklore. Today, these legendary beings stand as some of the most sophisticated and multifaceted creatures in Japanese mythology, embodying both spiritual power and moral ambiguity.

The evolution of Tengu mythology mirrors broader changes in Japanese religious and cultural history. When Buddhist teachings first arrived from China in the 6th century, they brought tales of the tiangou, dangerous dog-like spirits that opposed the dharma. As these stories took root in Japanese soil, they underwent a remarkable transformation. By the 12th century, Tengu had begun to assume their more familiar avian characteristics, appearing as crow-like beings called karasu tengu. This transformation continued through the medieval period, leading to the emergence of the distinctive long-nosed humanoid daitengu, often depicted wearing the garb of yamabushi—mountain ascetics who blended Buddhist and Shinto practices.

Physical descriptions of Tengu vary significantly, reflecting their complex hierarchy. The more numerous kotengu retain their crow-like features, with black feathers and beaks, while the powerful daitengu appear more human, distinguished by their long noses and red faces. Both types are typically portrayed wearing the formal robes of Buddhist priests or mountain ascetics, a choice of attire that speaks to their ambiguous relationship with organized religion.

Indeed, Tengu's connection to Buddhism presents one of their most fascinating contradictions. Early Buddhist texts denounced them as demons who opposed the dharma, yet over time, they came to be seen as protectors of certain temples and guardians of sacred mountains. This evolution reflects broader changes in Japanese religious thought, as native beliefs merged with imported Buddhism to create new synthetic traditions.

The martial aspects of Tengu lore deserve special attention. These beings are renowned as masters of combat, particularly swordsmanship and martial arts. Many famous warriors in Japanese history were said to have learned their skills from Tengu, training in secret mountain locations. The legendary swordsman Minamoto no Yoshitsune supposedly received his martial education from the Tengu of Mount Kurama, a story that highlights the beings' role as both teachers and tricksters.

Each major mountain region in Japan has its own Tengu traditions. Mount Kurama near Kyoto hosts the legendary Sōjōbō, king of all Tengu. Mount Takao, close to Tokyo, maintains active Tengu worship to this day, while Mount Atago hosts multiple Tengu shrines where believers still leave offerings. These regional variations share common elements while reflecting local historical and cultural conditions.

Modern interpretations of Tengu continue to evolve. Environmental groups sometimes invoke them as symbols of forest protection, drawing on their traditional role as mountain guardians. Martial arts schools reference Tengu teachings in their philosophical approaches, while popular culture regularly reimagines these beings for new audiences. Their enduring popularity speaks to their success in bridging ancient and modern worldviews, maintaining relevance across centuries of cultural change.

Perhaps most importantly, Tengu represent a distinctly Japanese approach to supernatural beings—neither purely good nor evil, but complex entities whose actions depend on context and human behavior. They punish arrogance yet teach wisdom, protect sacred spaces while testing human resolve, and maintain the delicate balance between the natural and supernatural worlds.

ONI
THE DEMONIC PARADOX
鬼

Region of Origin: All across Japan, from ancient mountains to haunted underworlds

Earliest Known Tales: Nara period (710–794)

Nature: Brutal, Loud, Occasionally Kind

Appearance: Massive ogre-like creature with red or blue skin, wild hair, horns, tiger-skin loincloth, and a spiked club (kanabō)

Unique Power: Super strength, terrifying roar, and the ability to smash almost anything—or carry away misbehaving children!

Danger Level: High... unless it's bean-throwing season—then they run!

From the sophisticated mountain spirits, we turn to what might be Japan's most iconic supernatural beings. The Oni stands as a testament to how yokai can evolve from simple forces of terror into complex cultural symbols. The very character used to write their name 鬼, originally meant "invisible spirit" or "hidden presence" before developing into its current meaning of "demon" or "ogre," reflecting the evolution of these beings in Japanese consciousness.

The physical appearance of Oni is striking and unmistakable. Towering over humans, these muscular beings sport one or more horns protruding from their heads, with skin in vivid shades of red, blue, or green. Their fierce faces feature sharp fangs and wild eyes, while their massive hands grip iron clubs called kanabō. Yet despite this fearsome appearance, Oni defy simple categorization as demons or monsters. Their role in Japanese mythology is far more nuanced, ranging from terrifying oni that devour humans to protective spirits that guard temples and dispense justice.

The origins of Oni beliefs trace back to prehistoric Japan, where they began as invisible forces that caused misfortune and disease. As Buddhism spread through Japan, these native spirits merged with Buddhist concepts of demons and karmic punishment. During the Heian period (794-1185), Oni became associated with the direction northeast, considered particularly unlucky, and elaborate ceremonies were performed at the imperial court to ward off their influence. This directional association survives today in the custom of throwing beans toward the northeast during Setsubun, the traditional beginning of spring.

Regional variations of Oni traditions reflect local histories and concerns. In Akita Prefecture, the Namahage tradition features Oni-like beings who visit homes during New Year's, frightening children into good behavior. Shikoku's Aya no Oni serves as a protective deity, while the Kijin of the Kinki region are associated with ancient agricultural rites. These regional differences show how Oni have been adapted to serve various social and cultural functions across Japan.

One of the most famous Oni tales centers on Shuten-dōji, the demon king of Mount Ōe. This complex narrative weaves together themes of power, corruption, and the thin line between human and demon. According to legend, Shuten-dōji began as a human child with supernatural powers who was rejected by society and eventually transformed into a powerful Oni. His defeat at the hands of the warrior Minamoto no Yorimitsu became a classic tale, but even in death, Shuten-dōji's severed head attempted one final bite at his conqueror, demonstrating the indomitable Oni spirit.

The role of Oni in Buddhist cosmology adds another layer to their character. Many serve as tormentors in Buddhist hells, administering punishments to sinful souls. However, this fearsome duty is seen not as evil but as a necessary function in maintaining cosmic order. Some Buddhist texts even suggest that Oni work under the direction of Emma-ō, the king of the underworld, as agents of ultimate justice rather than arbitrary violence.

In modern Japan, Oni continue to evolve and find new relevance. They feature prominently in festivals, where their fearsome aspects are celebrated rather than dreaded. The famous "Oni wa soto, fuku wa uchi" (Demons out, fortune in) cry during Setsubun has become a beloved tradition, transforming ancient terror into family entertainment. Popular culture regularly reinterprets Oni, sometimes casting them as misunderstood antiheroes or even romantic figures, showing how these ancient beings continue to adapt to changing social values.

KAWAAKAGO

THE RIVER BABY TRICKSTER

川赤子

Region of Origin: Mountain rivers and remote streams, especially in central and northern Japan

Earliest Known Tales: Edo period (1603–1868)

Nature: Deceptive, Mischievous

Appearance: Looks and cries like a human baby, often seen lying near the water's edge

Unique Power: Tricks kind-hearted people into picking it up—then suddenly becomes impossibly heavy and drags them into the river!

Danger Level: Cute but deadly—don't fall for the baby act!

From the imposing presence of Oni, we turn to a more insidious form of supernatural threat. Kawaakago represents how yokai can weaponize human compassion itself. The name, combining 川 (kawa, "river") with 赤子 (akago, "baby"), describes a spirit that exploits one of humanity's most basic instincts: the urge to help a crying infant.

The origins of Kawaakago legends are deeply rooted in Japan's historical relationship with its waterways. In an era when infant mortality was high and rivers claimed many young lives through drowning and flooding, these stories served multiple purposes. They helped communities process their grief, warned children about water dangers, and provided supernatural explanations for the heart-wrenching sounds that sometimes emerge from rushing waters at twilight.

Unlike many yokai who rely on fear or force, Kawaakago's power lies in manipulation of human empathy. Its signature technique—perfectly mimicking the cries of a distressed infant—targets what might be called humanity's most fundamental weakness: our instinct to protect children. When travelers hear these phantom cries near rivers or streams, especially during the dimming light of dusk, they face a terrible dilemma. To ignore a crying baby violates deep moral instincts, yet approaching the sound might lead to their doom.

The timing of Kawaakago's appearances is not random. Traditional accounts note that these spirits are most active during twilight hours, particularly during the rainy seasons when rivers run high and fast. This pattern reflects both practical dangers—when visibility near waterways is poorest—and supernatural beliefs about liminal times when the boundary between the human and spirit worlds grows thin.

Regional variations of the Kawaakago legend reflect local environmental conditions and tragic histories. In Hokkaido, stories tell of ice-breaking baby cries that lure people onto dangerous frozen rivers. Tohoku's versions often connect these spirits to spring floods, while Kyushu's coastal communities speak of Kawaakago appearing near tidal rivers, their cries mixing with the sound of incoming waves. These regional differences demonstrate how the basic legend adapted to address specific local hazards.

What makes Kawaakago particularly fascinating is its ambiguous nature. Unlike clearly malevolent yokai, this spirit's intentions remain unclear. Some versions of the legend suggest it simply

KAWAAKAGO

enjoys causing confusion and fear, while others propose a darker purpose—drawing victims to watery graves. A few tales even hint at a protective aspect, suggesting that the spirit's deceptions actually prevent people from wandering into more dangerous areas.

Modern interpretations of Kawaakago often focus on its psychological aspects. The legend taps into universal human experiences: the power of a baby's cry to override rational thought, the conflict between self-preservation and the duty to help others, and the way darkness and flowing water can play tricks on human senses. These elements help explain why the story continues to resonate even in an age when river dangers are better understood and controlled.

AKANAME
THE BATHROOM CLEANER
垢嘗

Region of Origin: All over Japan, especially in old, dirty bathhouses

Earliest Known Tales: Edo period (1603–1868)

Nature: Gross, Shy, Harmless

Appearance: Slender, goblin-like creature with long hair, sharp claws, and a super long tongue

Unique Power: Licks up grime, filth, and soap scum from dirty bathtubs—especially at night

Danger Level: Low… unless your bathroom is disgusting!

From the deadly deceptions of Kawaakago, we return to the domestic realm, where Akaname presents a different kind of unsettling presence. Its name tells its story directly: 垢 (aka, "filth") combined with 嘗め (name, "licking"), creating a compound that perfectly describes this peculiar yokai's primary activity. While not as immediately threatening as many of its supernatural peers, Akaname represents something perhaps more disturbing—the personification of domestic uncleanliness.

In the hierarchy of Japanese yokai, Akaname occupies a unique niche. Unlike the powerful Oni or the clever Tengu, this creature concerns itself solely with the mundane task of cleaning neglected bathrooms with its extraordinarily long tongue. Its appearance matches its humble role: a small, humanoid figure with reddish-brown skin, large bulbous eyes, and spindly limbs. Most distinctive is its tongue—an impossibly long, prehensile appendage capable of reaching the darkest corners of any bathroom.

The emergence of Akaname legends during the Edo period coincides with significant developments in Japanese urban life and public hygiene. As cities grew and public bathhouses became central to community life, new standards of cleanliness emerged. Akaname stories served as a form of social pressure, encouraging proper maintenance of both private and public facilities. After all, who would want their bathroom to become so dirty that it attracted a yokai?

The timing of Akaname's activities adds another layer to its legend. These creatures are said to appear late at night, when households are asleep. The sound of their tongue scraping against tiles and walls creates an eerie atmosphere, contributing to the unsettling nature of nighttime bathroom visits. This nocturnal aspect of the legend likely drew from real experiences—the strange sounds that old plumbing and settling buildings can make in the quiet hours.

Regional variations of the Akaname legend reflect different aspects of Japanese bathroom culture. In areas known for their public bathhouses, Akaname serves as a communal guardian of cleanliness. Rural traditions often connect it to outdoor facilities, where it becomes associated with proper waste management and environmental hygiene. Urban legends adapt the story to modern apartment buildings, where Akaname might travel between units through the plumbing system, checking on bathroom maintenance throughout the structure.

What makes Akaname particularly interesting is its ambiguous nature. Unlike many yokai who clearly mean harm, Akaname provides a service—albeit one that nobody wants to need.

AKANAME

Its presence serves as both a warning and a consequence of neglect. The creature's activities might be disgusting, but they highlight a fundamental truth: if humans won't maintain their spaces, nature (or in this case, supernatural forces) will find a way to restore balance.

Modern interpretations of Akaname often focus on its role as a metaphor for public health concerns. In an era of increased awareness about hygiene and disease transmission, the legend of a creature that appears in unclean bathrooms takes on new relevance. Some contemporary accounts even cast Akaname as a kind of supernatural health inspector, its presence serving as an indicator of facilities that need attention.

KEUKEGEN

THE FUZZBALL OF BAD LUCK
毛羽毛現

Region of Origin: Folk legends from across Japan

Earliest Known Tales: Edo period (1603–1868)

Nature: Shy, Ominous, Brings Illness

Appearance: A small, shaggy creature covered in long, messy hair—like a walking dustball with eyes

Unique Power: Appears in damp, moldy places and is said to bring bad luck, colds, and general ickiness

Danger Level: Medium—gross vibes and sniffles guaranteed!

While Akaname addresses visible uncleanliness, Keukegen manifests a more insidious form of domestic neglect. The name itself, 毛羽毛現, combines characters suggesting a manifestation (現) of hair (毛) and feathers (羽), perfectly describing this amorphous, fuzzy being that haunts neglected corners of Japanese homes. Unlike many yokai that actively seek human interaction, Keukegen's mere presence serves as both symptom and cause of household decay.

The physical form of this yokai reflects its nature as a creature born of neglect.

KEUKEGEN

Neither fully solid nor completely ethereal, Keukegen appears as a shifting mass of hair, dust, and feathers that can disperse and reform at will. Its semi-transparent appearance makes it difficult to spot directly, though its effects are all too noticeable. The creature's ability to move through the smallest gaps in a home's structure suggests an intimate connection with the domestic environment it inhabits.

Traditional beliefs link Keukegen directly to human health. Where these spirits gather, illness follows. Yet the relationship between cause and effect remains intriguingly ambiguous—does Keukegen bring sickness, or does it simply thrive in conditions that naturally lead to poor health? This uncertainty reflects a sophisticated understanding of the connection between environmental conditions and human wellbeing, clothed in supernatural garb.

The seasonal aspects of Keukegen activity provide insight into Japanese domestic life. These spirits are said to be most active during humid summers and the damp transition periods between seasons. This timing coincides with periods when Japanese homes are most vulnerable to mold and dust accumulation, suggesting that Keukegen legends helped encode practical knowledge about household maintenance within supernatural narratives.

Prevention methods for Keukegen infestation read like a manual of traditional Japanese household maintenance. Regular cleaning, proper ventilation, and allowing sunlight into dark corners all serve to ward off these unwanted guests. The practice of airing out homes and belongings during specific seasons—a custom that continues today—finds supernatural justification in Keukegen folklore. Even the traditional use of sacred salt for purification serves both spiritual and practical purposes, as salt's hygroscopic properties help control humidity.

Modern science offers intriguing parallels to Keukegen beliefs. The yokai's reported effects—respiratory problems, allergies, general malaise—mirror symptoms associated with poor

KEUKEGEN

indoor air quality and mold exposure. What our ancestors interpreted as a supernatural presence, we now understand as environmental health issues. Yet the fundamental wisdom remains the same: a clean, well-ventilated home is essential for human wellbeing.

Contemporary Japanese society continues to find relevance in Keukegen legends. As concerns about sick building syndrome and indoor air quality grow, this ancient yokai provides a cultural framework for discussing modern environmental health issues. The image of a malevolent dust bunny carrying illness resonates with current understanding of how airborne particles affect human health, demonstrating how traditional folklore can remain relevant across centuries of scientific advancement.

YOSUZUME

THE MYSTERIOUS NIGHT SPARROW

夜雀

Region of Origin: Mountain trails and forest paths, especially in western Japan

Earliest Known Tales: Edo period (1603–1868)

Nature: Mysterious, Mischievous, Potentially Ominous

Appearance: A small sparrow-like bird with glowing eyes and an eerie chirp—sometimes appears as a flock in the dark

Unique Power: Circles travelers at night, distracting or disorienting them—may be a warning of nearby yokai

Danger Level: Low… unless you're already lost!

From the indoor threats of Keukegen, we venture into the nocturnal wilderness where Yosuzume serves as nature's warning system. The name 夜雀 combines "night" (夜) with "sparrow" (雀), creating a deceptively simple title for a complex supernatural entity that bridges the natural and spiritual worlds.

Unlike many yokai that announce their presence with dramatic displays, Yosuzume's power lies in subtlety. Its song, heard in the gathering darkness, carries meanings that transcend ordinary bird calls. Those who know the old ways understand that when Yosuzume sings, it signals the presence of other, often more dangerous, supernatural beings. This role as harbinger places Yosuzume in a unique position within yokai hierarchy—not particularly powerful itself but intimately connected to forces that are.

The connection between Yosuzume and actual bird species reveals fascinating layers of Japanese natural history. The haunting notes of the Japanese Bush Warbler (ウグイス), the mysterious calls of the Brown-eared Bulbul (ヒヨドリ), and the nocturnal activities of the Japanese Night Heron (ゴイサギ) all contribute to the legend. These real birds' behaviors—particularly their tendency to call out at twilight or before dawn—helped shape beliefs about supernatural avian messengers.

Temporal patterns in Yosuzume appearances reflect traditional Japanese concepts about sacred time. The bird is most active during twilight hours, that liminal period when day transforms into night. This timing aligns with ancient beliefs about when the boundary between the mundane and spiritual worlds grows thin. Similarly, its activities peak during specific phases of the lunar cycle and at critical points in the traditional calendar, suggesting a deep connection to natural rhythms.

Geographic distribution of Yosuzume encounters creates a map of supernatural significance across Japan. The spirit appears most frequently near mountain passes, ancient forests, and temple grounds—places traditionally associated with supernatural activity. This pattern of appearance serves a practical purpose, warning travelers away from locations where they might encounter more dangerous yokai or natural hazards.

The relationship between Yosuzume and other yokai reveals complex supernatural politics. As messengers for Tengu, they participate in the governance of mountain realms. Their warnings sometimes precede appearances of Kappa or Oni, suggesting a role in maintaining boundaries between human and yokai

YOSUZUME

territories. Some accounts even describe them as part of a broader network of ghost birds that help maintain supernatural order.

Modern interpretations of Yosuzume often focus on its role as an environmental indicator. Just as actual birds serve as indicators of ecosystem health, Yosuzume's presence or absence might be seen as a measure of an area's spiritual vitality. This perspective has gained new relevance in contemporary discussions about environmental preservation and the maintenance of traditional sacred spaces.

BAKENEKO
THE SHAPE-SHIFTING CAT
化け猫

Region of Origin: All over Japan, especially in homes with very old or mistreated cats

Earliest Known Tales: Kamakura period (1185–1333)

Nature: Mysterious, Vengeful, Sometimes Helpful

Appearance: A regular house cat… until it grows huge, walks on two legs, and wears a kimono (sometimes)

Unique Power: Shape-shifts into humans, curses those who wrong it, dances with towels on its head, and may speak like a person

Danger Level: Depends on how nicely you treat your cat—be respectful or face the consequences!

From the warning songs of Yosuzume, we turn to a yokai that emerges from the heart of Japanese domestic life. The Bakeneko (化け猫) represents the mysterious transformation of the familiar into the fantastic, as ordinary housecats cross the threshold into supernatural power. The name itself tells the story—化け (bake, "transform") combined with 猫 (neko, "cat")—marking these beings as creatures of change and mystery.

Unlike many yokai who begin their existence as supernatural entities, Bakeneko emerge through a process of transformation that medieval Japanese society believed could happen to any household cat under the right conditions. Age serves as the primary catalyst—a cat that lives beyond thirteen years gains supernatural potential. Other factors contribute: the length of the tail (which may split to form two or more branches), the cat's weight, and most significantly, how humans treat their feline companions.

The powers attributed to Bakeneko reflect both feline nature and human anxieties about domestic boundaries. These transformed cats master human speech, perfect the art of shape-shifting, and develop the ability to create ghostly fireballs (hitodama) that float through the night air. Most disturbing of all, they can create perfect copies of recently deceased humans, often impersonating their former owners. This particular ability speaks to the intimate connection between cats and their human families—who else would know us well enough to create such a convincing imposture?

Historical records from the Edo period reveal fascinating intersections between Bakeneko legends and Buddhist practice. The prohibition against cat burial in certain Buddhist traditions led to complex funeral customs for felines, designed partly to prevent their transformation into yokai. These practices highlight the ambiguous position of cats in Japanese society—neither fully domestic nor fully wild, capable of moving between worlds just as their supernatural counterparts moved between forms.

Regional variations in Bakeneko stories reflect different aspects of human-feline relationships across Japan. In the Kanto region, tales focus on dancing cat spirits that entertain themselves in abandoned houses during the night. Kansai traditions emphasize Bakeneko haunting merchant households, perhaps reflecting the region's commercial culture. Kyushu's legends tell of fire-breathing cats, while Shikoku preserves stories of vengeful temple cats seeking

BAKENEKO

retribution for mistreatment.

The preventive measures traditionally used against Bakeneko transformation reveal much about historical attitudes toward cats. Some families would cut their cats' tails short, believing this would prevent supernatural development. Others insisted on cats wearing name collars inscribed with protective prayers. The most effective prevention, however, was simply treating cats with kindness and respect—a practice that benefited both natural and supernatural felines.

Modern Japanese culture continues to find new meanings in Bakeneko legends. Contemporary interpretations often focus on themes of loyalty and betrayal, examining how human treatment of animals reflects broader social values. The popularity of cat cafés and cat-themed media in Japan suggests an evolution in human-feline relationships, yet the ancient awareness of cats as creatures who walk between worlds persists in subtle ways.

TESSO

THE RAT KING OF THE TEMPLE
鉄鼠

Region of Origin: Enryaku-ji Temple on Mount Hiei, near Kyoto

Earliest Known Tales: Heian period (794–1185)

Nature: Vengeful, Swarming, Unholy

Appearance: A monstrous rat with a twisted monk-like face, surrounded by a horde of squeaking followers

Unique Power: Commands an army of plague-bearing rats that can chew through sacred temples and drive monks mad

Danger Level: High—pray your offerings are accepted… or prepare for a rodent rebellion!

While Bakeneko emerges from natural transformation, Tesso's origin lies in the darkness of human emotion. The tale of the Iron Rat (鉄鼠) begins not with supernatural elements, but with the very human story of a Buddhist priest named Raigo, whose righteous anger transformed him into one of Japan's most unusual yokai. His story serves as a powerful reminder that the line between human and supernatural can be crossed through the intensity of emotion alone.

The historical roots of Tesso's legend are firmly planted in the political soil of 10th century Japan. Raigo served as a respected priest at the prestigious Enryaku-ji temple complex atop Mount Hiei, a center of Buddhist power and learning. When the Imperial court sought his assistance in praying for the birth of an heir, Raigo agreed, requesting in return support for a new ordination platform at his temple. The success of his prayers—and the subsequent betrayal of the court's promise—would set in motion events that would transform a man of peace into a being of vengeance.

The physical manifestation of Tesso reflects both the nature of his transformation and the depth of his grudge. His new form combined human intelligence with the appearance of a massive rat, his body covered in iron-like fur that proved impervious to weapons. Most striking were his gleaming red eyes and iron teeth, capable of destroying sacred texts and religious artifacts. This focus on destroying Buddhist materials reveals the specific nature of his revenge—not merely against those who wronged him, but against the entire religious establishment he once served.

The army of rats that Tesso commanded adds another layer to his legend. These weren't ordinary rodents, but creatures enhanced by their master's supernatural power, their teeth as hard as metal and their movements coordinated with military precision. This aspect of the story might reflect historical concerns about the power of organized religious institutions, suggesting that even sacred spaces can harbor destructive forces.

The religious significance of Tesso's transformation extends beyond simple revenge. His story serves as a warning about the dangers of attachment and ego in spiritual practice. That a Buddhist priest—someone trained in the principles of non-attachment and compassion—could be so consumed by anger as to become a destructive yokai represents a powerful cautionary tale about the dangers of spiritual pride and the corruption of religious purpose.

Modern interpretations of Tesso's legend often focus on themes of institutional betrayal and the consequences of broken promises. His story resonates with contemporary discussions about power relationships between religious institutions and political authority, and the potential for righteous anger to transform into destructive force. The image of sacred texts being destroyed by iron-toothed rats serves as a potent metaphor for how corruption can eat away at institutional foundations.

ROKUROKUBI

THE NIGHT STRETCHER
ろくろ首

Region of Origin: All across Japan, especially in Edo-era ghost stories

Earliest Known Tales: Muromachi period (1336–1573)

Nature: Mysterious, Dual-natured (sometimes harmless, sometimes sinister)

Appearance: Looks like a normal human woman by day—but at night, her neck stretches impossibly long while she sleeps or prowls

Unique Power: Her neck stretches meters long to spy, scare, or snack on unsuspecting humans

Danger Level: Medium—don't assume your roommate's head is where you left it!

While Tesso's transformation was sudden and dramatic, Rokurokubi embodies a more subtle kind of metamorphosis. These yokai present an unsettling question: how well do we really know those who live among us? The name Rokurokubi (轆轤首) derives from the image of a potter's wheel (轆轤, rokuro) and neck (首, kubi), suggesting the smooth, mechanical extension of their most distinctive feature.

During daylight hours, Rokurokubi are indistinguishable from ordinary humans. They go about their daily lives, interact with neighbors, and maintain normal relationships, all while harboring their supernatural secret. It's only at night that their true nature emerges, as their necks stretch to impossible lengths, allowing their heads to wander freely while their bodies remain in bed. This duality of existence—normal by day, supernatural by night—speaks to deep-seated anxieties about identity and the unknown aspects of those closest to us.

The origin of their condition varies in different tellings. Some accounts present it as a curse, punishment for past misdeeds or broken religious vows. Others suggest it's an inherited trait, passed down through family lines, while still others frame it as a form of spiritual possession. The variety of origin stories reflects Japanese society's complex understanding of how ordinary people might find themselves transformed into supernatural beings.

The activities of Rokurokubi during their nighttime excursions reveal much about human nature. Many use their ability to spy on neighbors or eavesdrop on private conversations, suggesting a commentary on social surveillance and the human desire to know others' secrets. Some versions of the legend describe them consuming lamp oil or incense smoke, perhaps reflecting practical concerns about household resources mysteriously depleting during the night.

What makes Rokurokubi particularly fascinating is their often unconscious nature. Many are unaware of their nocturnal transformations, experiencing them only as dreams or strange sensations. This aspect of the legend speaks to universal experiences of disconnection between our waking and sleeping selves, and the fear that we might be capable of things beyond our conscious control.

The medical parallels to Rokurokubi legends are intriguing. Their reported symptoms—sleep disturbances, neck discomfort, and strange dreams—

ROKUROKUBI

mirror various sleep disorders recognized by modern medicine. The legends might have served as a way to explain sleep paralysis, out-of-body experiences, or other nocturnal phenomena that science has only recently begun to understand.

Contemporary interpretations of Rokurokubi often focus on themes of privacy, identity, and the secrets we keep from both others and ourselves.

In an age of social media and constant connectivity, the idea of a hidden supernatural nature that emerges only in private resonates with modern anxieties about public and private personas. The Rokurokubi's ability to extend beyond normal boundaries while remaining tethered to their original form provides a powerful metaphor for how we reach beyond ourselves while remaining bound by our nature.

HITOTSUME KOZO

THE ONE-EYED MONK IN TRAINING
一つ目小僧

Region of Origin: All across Japan, especially temple towns and mountain paths

Earliest Known Tales: Edo period (1603–1868)

Nature: Playful, Harmless, Surprising

Appearance: A childlike monk with a bald head, traditional robes… and one giant eyeball in the center of his face

Unique Power: Startles people by popping up suddenly—often just for fun! Sometimes delivers messages from the yokai world

Danger Level: Low—more of a jump-scare enthusiast than a threat!

Unlike the hidden nature of Rokurokubi, Hitotsume Kozo wears his supernatural nature plainly on his face. This one-eyed child monk represents one of the more unusual entries in the yokai pantheon, combining religious imagery with an almost playful approach to human interaction. His name tells his story directly: 一つ目 (hitotsume, "one eye") combined with 小僧 (kozo, "young Buddhist monk"), creating an image that is both unsettling and somehow endearing.

The appearance of Hitotsume Kozo precisely balances the familiar with the strange. In the form of a young Buddhist monk, he would have been a common sight in traditional Japan, where many families sent sons to temples for education and training. Yet his single eye, centered in his face like a cyclops, marks him as clearly otherworldly. This combination of the mundane and the mysterious reflects the yokai's unique position as a bridge between human and supernatural realms.

Historical context places the emergence of Hitotsume Kozo legends firmly within Japan's complex religious landscape. During periods when Buddhist temples served as centers of education, the sight of young monks-in-training was commonplace in urban areas. These child monks, often serving as messengers and performing minor duties, were integral to temple operations. Hitotsume Kozo appears to be a supernatural reflection of these young servants, though his duties extend beyond mere temple errands.

Unlike many yokai who actively seek to harm or trick humans, Hitotsume Kozo's interactions tend toward the mischievous rather than the malicious. He often appears suddenly in quiet alleyways or around corners, startling passersby with his unexpected presence. Yet these encounters, while surprising, usually end without harm—the shock of seeing his single eye seems to be entertainment enough for this peculiar spirit.

The symbolism of the single eye carries deep significance in Japanese folklore. In many traditions, supernatural beings with unusual numbers of eyes or other features represent beings who can see beyond normal human perception. Hitotsume Kozo's central eye might suggest an ability to perceive spiritual truths directly, fitting for a being associated with Buddhist training and wisdom.

Regional variations of Hitotsume Kozo legends reflect different aspects of urban religious life. In Tokyo, he's known for appearing near temple grounds and in narrow streets. Kyoto's

HITOTSUME KOZO

versions often connect him to specific historical temples, while rural areas cast him as a wandering spirit who tests the kindness of villagers. These regional differences highlight how supernatural beliefs adapted to local conditions and concerns.

Modern interpretations often focus on Hitotsume Kozo's role as a reminder of childhood innocence and religious education. In contemporary Japan, where traditional Buddhist training has become less common, he serves as a connection to historical practices and values. His continued presence in popular culture, often in a more lighthearted form than many yokai, suggests a nostalgic view of traditional religious education and childhood spiritual experiences.

YAMA UBA
THE MOUNTAIN WITCH
山姥

Region of Origin: Deep mountains and remote villages of Japan, especially in the Tōhoku and Kantō regions

Earliest Known Tales: Muromachi period (1336–1573)

Nature: Ambiguous—both nurturing and deadly

Appearance: An old woman with wild hair, tattered kimono, and a hungry glint in her eyes—often seen with a baby on her back

Unique Power: Shape-shifts, conjures storms, devours travelers—or raises legendary heroes like Kintarō

Danger Level: Variable—she might feed you soup… or feed on you!

Our journey through Japan's supernatural realm concludes with perhaps its most complex figure. Yama Uba (山姥), the mountain crone, embodies the fundamental duality found throughout yokai lore. Her name simply combines "mountain" (山) with "old woman" (姥), yet this straightforward title belies the intricate nature of a being who can be both nurturing mother and deadly predator, wise teacher and fearsome monster.

Unlike urban yokai who haunt specific locations or domestic spirits bound to households, Yama Uba's domain encompasses the entire mountain wilderness. She appears where civilization meets untamed nature: remote trails, hidden valleys, and mysterious forests. Her territory reflects her nature—neither fully human nor completely wild, but existing in the space between these realms. Like the mountains themselves, she can be either welcoming or deadly, depending on how humans approach her.

The physical appearance of Yama Uba varies with her mood and intent. To lost travelers seeking shelter, she might appear as a gentle grandmother offering warmth and food in her mountain hut. To those who enter her domain with arrogance or disrespect, she reveals her more terrifying aspect—flowing white hair, a mouth that can unhinge like a snake's, and an appetite for human flesh. This transformation mirrors the mountain environment itself, which can shift from serene beauty to lethal danger in moments.

Perhaps the most fascinating aspect of Yama Uba lore is her role in the legend of Kintaro, the golden boy. In this tale, she appears not as a monster but as a nurturing foster mother, raising an abandoned child who would become one of Japan's greatest folklore heroes. This maternal aspect of Yama Uba suggests deeper truths about nature's dual capacity to both sustain and destroy life. Her careful education of Kintaro in the ways of the mountain demonstrates how wilderness, properly respected, can be a source of strength and wisdom.

The seasonal patterns of Yama Uba's activity reflect traditional understanding of mountain life. Winter finds her isolated in deep snows, growing hungry and dangerous. Spring sees her gathering mountain herbs and teaching their use to respectful students. Summer brings abundance and relative benevolence, while autumn heralds a return to more aggressive hunting behavior. These cycles mirror both natural rhythms and the practical

YAMA UBA

knowledge needed for survival in Japan's mountain regions.

Modern interpretations of Yama Uba often focus on environmental themes. Her legends remind us that nature deserves respect rather than conquest, that wisdom can be found in wild places, and that the line between nurturing and destructive forces often depends on human attitude and behavior. In an age of environmental crisis, her story resonates with contemporary concerns about wilderness preservation and sustainable interaction with natural spaces.

The enduring power of Yama Uba's legend lies in its refusal to settle for simple categorization. She is neither good nor evil, neither fully human nor completely supernatural. Like the mountains themselves, she simply is— a force to be respected, a teacher to those who listen, and a warning to those who would take nature's power lightly. In this complexity, she serves as a fitting conclusion to our exploration of yokai, embodying the sophisticated way Japanese folklore approaches the supernatural world.

REFERENCES

PUBLICATIONS

ASHKENAZI, MICHAEL. (2003). Handbook of Japanese Mythology. ABC-CLIO.

CASAL, U.A. (1959). "The Tengu". Folklore, Vol 70, No. 4.

DAVISSON, ZACK (2017). Kaibyō: The Supernatural Cats of Japan. Chin Music Press.

DAVIS, F. HADLAND (1913). Myths & Legends of Japan. George G. Harrap & Company.

FOSTER, MICHAEL DYLAN (2015). The Book of Yōkai: Mysterious Creatures of Japanese Folklore. University of California Press.

HEARN, LAFCADIO (1904). "Rokuro-kubi". In Kwaidan: Stories and Studies of Strange Things. Houghton Mifflin Company.

IWASAKA, MICHIKO & TOELKEN, BARRE (1994). Ghosts and the Japanese: Cultural Experience in Japanese Death Legends. Utah State University Press.

MEYER, MATTHEW (2012). The Night Parade of One Hundred Demons. Self-Published.

MIZUKI, SHIGERU (1968). Mizuki's Yokai Encyclopaedia. Kodansha.

REIDER, NORIKO (2010). Japanese Demon Lore: Oni from Ancient Times to the Present. Utah State University Press.

REIDER, NORIKO (2021). Mountain Witches: Yamauba. Utah State University Press.

SEKIEN, TORIYAMA (1776–1781). Gazu Hyakki Yagyō (The Illustrated Night Parade of a Hundred Demons). Edo Period Prints.

TYLER, ROYALL (1987). Japanese Tales. Pantheon Books.

WYATT, DANIEL J. (2017). "Creatures of Myth and Modernity: Shōjō (Orangutans) as Exotic Animals". New Voices in Japanese Studies, 9, pp.71–93.

ANIME AND GAMES

AYAKASHI: SAMURAI HORROR TALES (Anime, 2006). Toei Animation.

CASTLEVANIA: ARIA OF SORROW (Video Game, 2003). Konami.

DEMON SLAYER: KIMETSU NO YAIBA (Manga/Anime, 2016–present). Koyoharu Gotōge, Shueisha.

DORORO (Anime, 2019). MAPPA/Tezuka Productions.

GEGEGE NO KITARŌ (Anime, 1960s–present). Shigeru Mizuki, Toei Animation.

GHOST STORIES (Anime, 2000). Studio Pierrot.

NARUTO (Manga/Anime, 1999–2014). Masashi Kishimoto, Shueisha.

NIOH & NIOH 2 (Video Games, 2017–2020). Team Ninja, Koei Tecmo.

NURA: RISE OF THE YOKAI CLAN (Manga/Anime, 2008–2010). Hiroshi Shiibashi, Shueisha.

ONIMUSHA: WARLORDS (Video Game, 2001). Capcom.

POM POKO (Film, 1994). Studio Ghibli, directed by Isao Takahata.

THE LEGEND OF ZELDA: MAJORA'S MASK (Video Game, 2000). Nintendo.

TOUHOU PROJECT – IMPERISHABLE NIGHT (Video Game, 2004). Team Shanghai Alice.

YO-KAI WATCH (Game/Anime, 2013–present). Level-5.

Printed in Great Britain
by Amazon